# The Fabian Socie.

The Fabian Society is Britain's leading left of centre think tank and
political society, committed to creat........litical ideas and policy
debates which can sl...........sive politics.

With over 300 Fabio............
plays an unparalleleu .................,.. influence policy
debates at the highest le... with vigorous grassroots debate among our
growing membership of over 7000 people, 70 local branches meeting
regularly throughout Britain and a vibrant Young Fabian section
organising its own activities. Fabian publications, events and ideas
therefore reach and influence a wider audience than those of any
comparable think tank. The Society is unique among think tanks in
being a thriving, democratically-constituted membership organisation,
affiliated to the Labour Party but organisationally and editorially
independent.

For over 120 years Fabians have been central to every important
renewal and revision of left of centre thinking. The Fabian commitment
to open and participatory debate is as important today as ever before
as we explore the ideas, politics and policies which will define the next
generation of progressive politics in Britain, Europe and around the
world. Find out more at **www.fabian-society.org.uk**

Fabian Society
11 Dartmouth Street
London SW1H 9BN
www.fabian-society.org.uk

Fabian ideas
Series editor: Jonathan Heawood

First published March 2005

ISBN 0 7163 0614 X
ISSN 1746-1146

British Library Cataloguing in Publication data.
A catalogue record for this book is available from the British Library.


Printed by Bell & Bain, Glasgow

# Must Politics Disappoint?

by
**Meg Russell**

## About the author

Dr Meg Russell is a Senior Research Fellow at the Constitution Unit, School of Public Policy, University College London. She worked for the Labour Party from 1996 to 1998 and was later seconded as Special Adviser to Robin Cook in his role as Leader of the House of Commons from 2001 to 2003. She is a member of the Fabian Society Executive, and writes here in a personal capacity.

# Contents

# Acknowledgements

I would like to thank all those who have offered help and encouragement in the preparation of this pamphlet, and particularly those who read and commented on earlier drafts. These include Philip Carter, Robin Cook, Alf Dubs, Guy Lodge, Neal Lawson, Jean Seaton and Ben Seyd. Thanks also to those in the Fabian office, including Adrian Harvey, Research Director when the pamphlet was commissioned, and particularly Sunder Katwala and Jonathan Heawood whose advice and support enabled it to be brought to completion. Special thanks to Sir Bernard Crick, both for his comments on earlier drafts and also for providing the preface.

# Preface
## Bernard Crick

Must politics disappoint? Meg Russell chooses her words carefully. In Britain today, 'disappoint' is the *mot juste*. No sense in being melodramatic: 'politics under threat'; 'politics in decay'; 'politics despised'; 'politics in crisis' — though all of these might have passed through the author's mind. No, just plainly and sadly 'disappoint'.

Personally, I feel an inner rage every day at the disparity between what is promised and what is delivered, between what is possible and what is happening, between the 'is' and the 'ought'; and that the level of rational public debate is now at what any historian or honest student of politics must recognise as a unique low since the 1880s.

Distrust of politicians could, indeed, lead to a distrust of the whole political process. Opinion polls show that politicians now rank below journalists in the public mind. Measures of participation reveal little beyond 'cheque-book' participation in both parties and pressure groups. A long time ago I annoyed the management committee of my local party by calling myself 'a banker's order of the party'. But that is now the norm. It is a long time since anyone came knocking at my door.

Meg Russell is serious and not melodramatic. She probes deep below our fashionable friend (in different guises) 'the democratic deficit'. For she sees that democracy (if it is not to be, in de Tocqueville's phrase, 'the tyranny of the majority' and its tutelary leaders) must presuppose the political process itself—the necessary compromising of differing interests and values that is the hallmark of free societies, albeit hopefully creative compromises that should add not subtract, bit by bit, to the general good. Too many people now are uninterested in politics, or sceptical, even cynical, about the whole process. Fiddling with making it easier to vote misses the point, is just cosmetic; people must want to vote.

So the author is kind to begin her calm analysis of the troubles of our time by recalling the argument of my *In Defence of Politics*. But back then in 1962 I had it easy. During the Cold War there was a clear contrast between totalitarian regimes and free political regimes, even if none of the latter are ever fully democratic by ideal standards. Russell deals subtly with the more perplexing shadow-land of a nominally democratic polity that partly creates and partly mirrors public disillusion with the political process itself. Has strong attachment to the ideas of representative government and active citizenship become swamped in general gratitude for governments that tolerate, even encourage, an unrestrained and enthusiastic consumerism? It is as if Michael Young had never written his prescient satire of 1958, *The Rise of the Meritocracy*—some may remember and some take care to forget. The Prime Minister's speech-writers have unfortunately used this coinage as if the positive ideal of a choice, choice, choice society.

I have read this timely, salutary, and wise pamphlet and meditation with great intellectual excitement and found in it, at the end, some grounds for political hope, if our leaders have eyes and ears, and if what is left of the party stirs itself, not angrily but thoughtfully, and persistently.

# Introduction
## Must Politics Disappoint?

There is a widespread belief that politics is in trouble. Barely a day goes by when we are not reminded that trust in political institutions is low, and that people are turning away from the mainstream political parties. We have become accustomed to the idea that people feel let down by politicians of all parties. Electoral turnout, in particular, is a big concern. At the forthcoming general election the question 'how many will vote?' will be asked at least as often as 'who will win?'

Since the drop in turnout in 2001 there has been a rash of interest in what encourages political participation. Politicians ask how trust in the political process can be restored; and in response there has been no shortage of proposals for reform. These include changing the electoral system for the House of Commons, electing the House of Lords, making it easier to vote electronically or by post and lowering the voting age to 16. If all else fails, some suggest, voting should be made compulsory.

This pamphlet takes a different approach, suggesting that the culture of politics is itself in large part to blame for the public's disappointment with the political process. Whilst institutional and structural reforms may have their merits, they ignore the deeper cultural reasons for disengagement. Their impact on curbing the problem will therefore be, at best, limited. Instead we need to ask bigger questions about why politics now seems to be so out of step with modern life.

This pamphlet argues that we have simply never adjusted to the challenges of mass politics. We now have a better educated and wealthier electorate — as a result of changes that mass democracy, and particularly parties of the left, actively sought to bring about. Meanwhile, there has been an explosion of outlets for political communication. These changes hold great potential for creating a new and more engaged politics; yet the opportunities they offer have largely passed us by. Instead, the ways that our political culture has adapted itself to modern life have, over time, conspired to erode faith in political rule. Politicians and the media fail to communicate the very essence of politics — that it is about negotiation and compromise, difficult choices, and taking decisions together as a society — to the extent that it is now seen as something largely divorced from everyday life, where politicians are expected to 'deliver', and increasingly talk their profession down rather than up, within a media environment that is hostile rather than supportive.

New developments have combined with British political tradition to create a potent cocktail that helps to undermine the political profession. Our long-established adversarial culture has combined with the 'permanent campaign' to encourage politicians to drive down trust in their opponents — thereby perpetuating mistrust in politics itself. Meanwhile, the culture of modern consumerism has helped set expectations that politics can, in reality, never meet.

Similarly, new and more sophisticated techniques for gauging public opinion have enabled political parties to tailor their messages to citizens' concerns in increasingly subtle ways. Yet this has discouraged them from presenting the big choices facing society, which are the very things that politics exists to address. A failure to open genuine debates with citizens about these issues, and to discuss who has responsibility for bringing change about, means that politicians are bound to disappoint. At the same time they are subject to pressure from single issue groups (often cited optimistically as the manifestation of a new form of political engagement), which themselves never have to face the difficult task of balancing competing demands. As a result, citizens appear increasingly separate from these processes, and can blame others for the perception that politics 'fails'. The modern media—though not solely responsible—has played a key part in feeding all of these problems.

Some have suggested that political disengagement should not give us cause for concern. Britain is a stable society and, since similar patterns are visible in other advanced democracies, complacency, or even apathy, could be considered a sign of success. After all, electoral turnout and identification with political parties has fallen in most OECD countries since the 1950s and 1960s.[1] Many big social changes, including declining class loyalties and new family and leisure patterns, are associated with these developments. In the absence of war or catastrophe, when politics is broadly delivering what people want, citizens may simply feel free to ignore it.

Yet the problem in Britain seems more serious than that, given the way in which falling participation is linked to a decline in trust. In the last 30 years the proportion of people saying that they trust government has more than halved, and a recent survey found that only one per cent of respondents said they trusted politicians 'a great deal'.[2] Combined with falling electoral turnout, these figures suggest that the legitimacy of our institutions is now at risk.

This pamphlet therefore does not suggest that we should be relaxed about political disengagement. Nor does it pretend that there are easy answers. We must face up to some big cultural challenges if we are to turn politics around. Only a conscious effort by the political classes to create a new and more honest politics, that seeks to build on the social advances we have made, will have any real chance of success. Only by having a frank conversation with people as citizens, rather than consumers, can politics hope to survive.

The sections that follow explore these issues in more depth, considering both how disappointment in the political process has grown and how it can be reversed. Six key factors are identified, each of which is illustrated by examples drawn from current debates. The final section then draws together a discussion of the possible antidotes. A key conclusion is that structural change alone can never be enough. A concerted effort by all those engaged in the political process to change their behaviour is now essential if faith in politics is to be restored. This requires a cross-party initiative by concerned politicians, and changes from journalists, other groups and citizens themselves.

A central argument in the pamphlet is that many of our problems stem from our having forgotten what politics is there for, and why it is beneficial. This applies not just to citizens, but also to politicians, and the media. Before discussing the cultural factors undermining politics it is thus important to pause and ask a prior question. What exactly is politics anyway? And what does it seek to achieve?

## Politics and the alternatives

It may appear odd to ask what politics is. It is tempting to respond by paraphrasing Herbert Morrison's famous definition of socialism and say that politics is simply 'what politicians do'. This, at any rate, seems to be how the majority of British people now understand the term. However, such a view simply reflects the growing sense of separation between the public and their politicians. We have lost sight of what politics is for, why it is beneficial, and what the alternatives are. Indeed the Electoral Commission has recently concluded that 'many people seem to see "politics" as an obstruction to, rather than the means of, proper government of the country'.[3] If this trend is to be reversed we need to understand and nurture — indeed celebrate — the thing that is politics.

In his seminal *In Defence of Politics* (1962), Bernard Crick contemplated the Cold War alternatives to political rule. He proposed that politics is 'the activity by which differing interests within a given unit of rule are conciliated by giving them a share in power in proportion to their importance to the welfare and the survival of the whole community'.[4] This principle was in short supply in many countries around Europe at the time that Crick was writing. These included not only the 'Eastern Bloc', but also the dictatorships in Spain and Portugal. So Crick

6

defended politics against alternatives such as nationalism, ideological dogma, technology, and even the tyranny of the majority.

In examining politics in relation to six key factors in modern life, this pamphlet consciously adopts a similar structure to that of Crick. The factors considered here are seemingly more benign than the stark alternatives that he offered, but in some ways this also makes them more challenging. In today's Europe at least, politics seems to have won the battle against the original threats that he identified. This in itself has made us less conscious of the alternatives to political rule, and less assiduous in its defence. Yet, it is argued here, politics in modern Britain still needs defending — it is only that the threats to it are different from those which went before.

Politics is, in short, a process by which complex societies take decisions. In such societies there are many different interests to be balanced. These may span, for example, fundamental ethnic, religious, economic, class or geographic divides. In Britain today they also include the needs of the old versus the young, urban dwellers versus those in the countryside, employers versus unions, parents versus the childless. At the more micro level they include car drivers versus users of public transport, savers versus borrowers, homeowners versus tenants, and so on. And of course they include the desires of those holding different sets of ideological beliefs: supporters of greater redistribution of wealth, liberal free markets, environmental protection, intervention in international conflicts, or a greater or lesser role for the state.

To maintain a stable and fair society it is the job of politicians to take account of these competing interests in deciding public policy. Politics is fundamentally a process of negotiation and compromise. Those participating are not just professional politicians, but the interest groups, parties, lobbyists, campaign groups and of course voters who take part in negotiations over policy. This deliberation and negotiation sets political rule apart from autocratic or totalitarian systems.

In diverse societies with well educated and demanding electorates it is perhaps remarkable that this process operates as smoothly as it does.

It is true that even when competing demands are balanced and political decisions taken they are not always universally welcomed. Given a multitude of perspectives and interests there will always be frustrated losers. But by and large the system by which conclusions are reached is respected, the law is complied with, and divisions rarely descend into disorder and violence. Episodes such as the fuel protests in 2000 and the riots in Bradford and Burnley in 2001 offer recent counterexamples in Britain. The fact that such events achieve high prominence is testament to their rarity. But they nonetheless demonstrate the potential dangers when trust in our institutions breaks down.

The ability of politics to contain and manage differences is undoubtedly something to be celebrated. It is true that political rule does not allow everyone to get what they want. Yet the alternatives are markedly worse. If respect for different perspectives cannot be maintained societies will be faced with 'either anarchy or the tyranny of single truths'.[5] There are plenty of examples of both of these worldwide. Rwanda, Kosovo and Bosnia all remind us where the inability to maintain toleration may lead in the extreme. Elsewhere the globe has been littered with regimes that chose to avoid managing differences by instead suppressing the interests of certain groups.

A civilised and diverse society is thus utterly dependent on politics. The process when seen in historical perspective is 'a great and civilizing human activity' and 'not just a necessary evil; it is a realistic good'.[6] Politics enables us to respect differing positions in a plural society, and to resolve conflicts peaceably. But, given the evidence quoted above about attitudes in Britain, it seems that few would now agree that it is something to celebrate. In reflecting on this it is noteworthy that electoral turnout remains highest among those who lived through the second world war, and those who were brought up in its aftermath. Among younger groups, less familiar with the alternatives to pluralism, the sense that you can choose to opt out of participation has spread.

None of this is to suggest that our political system is perfect or that we should be complacent about the need to improve it. Nor does it suggest that we stand on the brink of civil disobedience or totalitarianism. But a reflection on the alternatives does demonstrate the importance of protecting and nurturing the ethos of politics—negotiation, compromise and toleration—within modern public life. If we take these traditions for granted we do not know how fragile they may prove to be. Whilst the ethos of politics may have been undermined only slowly and inadvertently, there is a real danger that the legitimacy of our democratic institutions is now being eroded. We must therefore examine the factors that may undermine the ethos of politics and contribute to public disappointment in it and seek to manage them carefully, considering where cultural changes may be necessary. That is the task of this pamphlet.

# 1 | Politics and Consumerism

It is difficult to find anything more antithetical to the culture of politics than the contemporary culture of consumerism. While politics is about balancing diverse needs to benefit the public interest, consumerism is about meeting the immediate desires of the individual. While politics requires us to compromise and collaborate as citizens, consumerism emphasises unrestrained individual freedom of choice. While politics recognises that there are always resource constraints, modern consumerism increasingly encourages us to believe that we can have it all now.

The development of mass politics has been accompanied by—and indeed has actively facilitated—mass consumerism. It is in large part due to the achievements of the left in the early twentieth century that access to quality goods and services is no longer restricted to the privileged few. And whilst the Thatcher governments of the 1980s may have promoted the market ethic and the philosophy of competitive individualism, it is the economic stability of more recent years that has enabled mass consumerism to reach new levels. As memories fade of the blight of unemployment and home repossessions, people gain greater economic confidence.

As a consequence we are now seeing increasing levels of consumer debt, encouraged by banks, credit card providers and advertisers who seek to convince us that spending more money will bring us the gratification that we seek. Given the wealth and confidence to enjoy our purchasing power, we increasingly find our identity through what we buy—be it clothes, mobile phones, home furnishings or holidays—rather than what we contribute to society. In order to maintain our status we are encouraged to upgrade, constantly. We spend money on carefully branded bottles of mineral water when a largely identical (and far more environmentally benign) alternative is freely available through the tap. All of these developments have led the present era to be dubbed the age of 'turboconsumerism'.

Whilst the consumer culture includes many freedoms that we can celebrate, this particular product of Labour's economic success may in its own way be contributing to the declining belief in the political. The culture of consumerism is a major challenge to the collectivist ethic upon which politics depends. Politics in large part exists to regulate markets and deliver what they can't. The job of the politician is to face difficult choices, to balance interests, and ultimately sometimes to say 'no'. Many political questions can only be resolved if citizens take greater responsibility, and put limitations on their own freedoms in order to benefit the public good. Sometimes groups with competing interests simply have to compromise. The more the market ethic becomes ubiquitous, the more people will lose touch with these basic truths. They may make demands on the basis of what they believe they have 'paid' for (through their taxes) rather than exercising the constraint necessary for the system to cater effectively for all.

Politicians have long sought to respond to the consumer culture. Under the Conservatives, users were encouraged to be more demanding, and public services sought to create more 'businesslike' relationships. Thus for example those travelling on the (still public) London tube have long been addressed as 'customers' rather than 'passengers'. In the privatised services the shift in culture was even more stark. But encouraging such changes has not been restricted to politicians from the right. Hence Labour's current debates about the merits of personalising traditional public services to introduce wider 'choice' for users, which have caused unease to many on the left.

It is inarguable that users of public services should be treated efficiently, with courtesy and respect. Similarly it would be absurd not to use new technologies to give greater flexibility to NHS patients in choosing appointment times. Yet the wholesale adoption of the language of consumer markets in public services, including the notion that users can 'shop around', carries the risk that the spheres of citizenship and private individual gain become ever more blurred. In this way expectations may be set which are simply doomed to fail, and can only feed disappointment in politics and the political.

This pamphlet's core concern is not with the merits of introducing market mechanisms into public services — on which much has been written elsewhere[1] — but on the serious implications which the consumerist culture holds for politics itself. In his recent book, *Decline of the Public*, David Marquand argued that trust in state services and the professions was corroded by a belief — drawn from 'public choice' theory in economics — that workers in these fields were driven by self interest rather a commitment to the greater public good.[2] This belief underlay the Conservative drives to introduce market ethics within public services — which in turn helped corrode the public service ethos that did exist. Many now argue that restoring faith in the public service ethic may prove essential to retaining public support for these services, given the necessary limitations on their capacity (themselves largely created by the tax levels that citizens are willing to pay). But it may prove equally important to maintaining faith in politics itself. If a consumer ethos drowns out a public sector ethos in our services, politics would be left dangerously isolated, as the only sphere where a different set of rules applies. Even if some public services prove able to survive a new market relationship with citizens, politics, by its very nature, cannot.

There is a growing tendency in modern politics to appeal to voters as consumers, using the familiar language of the market when a choice between different policy options must be faced. It is not hard to find evidence of politicians responding to the consumer culture by conceptualising political dilemmas in these terms. In February 2003, for example, Transport Secretary Alistair Darling gave a speech to the AA with the central argument that the government should 'treat motorists as customers'. Yet whilst motorists may be demanding users of public services (i.e., roads), they are certainly not customers. A motorist who behaved as such would take as much from the system as their financial means allowed, without necessarily having regard to the needs of others. As road space is limited, far from being encouraged to act selfishly, car drivers' duties as citizens must be stressed if we are to manage congestion and pollution. Under this ethic they would, whenever possible, leave their cars at home. The same logic applies across many other areas of public policy, particularly in the environmental field — for example with respect to air travel and airport expansion, household waste and recycling, noise and other forms of anti-social behaviour. In these fields, only an emphasis on citizenship, rather than consumption, can bring about a better quality of life for all.

In seeking to manage demand and encourage responsibility, politicians now increasingly use price mechanisms, so that users make decisions on economic grounds. Road pricing, for example — which has worked in London and is therefore likely to spread — is used to limit traffic growth. Similarly, it has been proposed that households should be charged for refuse collection by weight, to encourage recycling and waste minimisation. Yet whilst these models may have some success, they are a further example of edging the citizen relationship towards a consumer one. Rather than citizens being encouraged to engage with moral choices about the impact of their behaviour, such decisions are reduced to economic transactions. In this way they may breed resentment rather than responsibility. More political dilemmas are loaded onto the politicians, whilst the 'consumers' are left simply protesting about the cost. Thus not only are price mechanisms regressive (as they are dependent on the ability to pay), but they also bring other problems.

Research suggests that the consumer model is far less effective in changing behaviour than partnership-based models in which individuals are persuaded of the benefits of changing their behaviour.[3] Pricing may have its place, but if politicians' response to the consumer culture is to deny that there are tough choices (rather than just consumer choices) to be made, they are effectively denying the nature of political rule itself. This, in turn, can only help to weaken its hold.

The extent to which the consumer approach to politics has fed through to the public was recently illustrated with respect to the Asian tsunami disaster. For days the media celebrated the generosity of the British public in donating to charity, contrasted with the 'meanness' of the politicians with regard to pledging government funds. However, politicians' ability to provide aid depends on their ability to raise this through taxation. Government money is not separate from our money: they are one and the same thing. On this occasion the politicians themselves accepted the media analysis, and Tony Blair finally promised to 'match' the donations the public had made. Yet the degree of public compassion had provided a rare opportunity for government to open a dialogue about the use of public resources, and to ask people collectively how they wished to see their money spent. Instead the opportunity was lost, and the gulf between politicians and the public gently edged wider.

For politics to survive it must therefore unashamedly carve out its own sphere, driven by the rules of citizenship. These demand that everyone is of equal worth and that compromise is sometimes necessary in order to maximise the common good. Such a culture depends on appealing to different human instincts from those which the market seeks to satisfy, and politics is needed to create these countervailing pressures and incentives. This is not out of step with the public mood. Whilst consumption can boost our happiness in many ways, all the evidence is that ever more of it is not sufficient to improve quality of life. Just as people rejected the old choice of 'any colour so long as it's black', there is growing unease at the offer of 'anything you want so long as it can be delivered by the market'. What many people desire is more time to be with friends and family, more courtesy from strangers, a cleaner environment or a more peaceful and secure world. As one recent Fabian author has suggested, they want a 'better choice of choice'.[4] Only politics and a culture of citizenship can deliver this.

An engaged politics requires that difficult choices are openly faced and discussed with citizens. Rather than creating the impression that they can respond to unlimited public demands, politicians have a responsibility to be frank with the electorate about the constraints within which they operate. They need to communicate that change is a collective enterprise, in which we are engaged together, and that some matters can be dealt with by neither the market nor the state but depend on responsible action by individuals. In short, politicians need to remind us what politics is for, and why it depends on an ethos that is different from that of the market.

Many of the signs for a more frank and engaged politics are good. Research shows that honesty is consistently the most highly rated characteristic of politicians—scoring far higher than competence or efficiency.[5] And when the language of difficult choices was deployed over the 2002 budget, the government won general public support for rises in National Insurance contributions to boost Health Service funding. But engagement such as this should not be a one-off event. An ongoing dialogue between government and citizens about the link between revenues and public service provision could help build a greater sense of responsibility and ownership of public policy decisions. The present response often acknowledges that we are a wealthier society, where everyone understands the rule of the market. But it too often fails to recognise that we are also a better educated society, one benefit of which should be an increased ability to understand and engage with mature political debates. If the electorate concludes that the current level of taxation is roughly their limit—as most politicians assume—then debate should focus on the best use of existing resources. Evidence from overseas suggests that this approach can promote engagement and lead to better decisions.[6] In presenting choices, and talking about improvements in public provision, politicians therefore need to communicate their belief that choice, flexibility and responsiveness are not simply imports from the private sector. Politics can and should disengage from the language of markets, and openly define itself as a realm in which different values prevail.

Creating a comfortable sphere within which politics can operate may, however, require more than this. It is difficult to see how politics can survive as a small island in the middle of a rampant consumer culture. Whilst Margaret Thatcher famously used 'pocketbook economics' to persuade the public of the merits of controlling the public sector deficit, it is challenging for politicians to persuade voters that there are limits to public resources, and that individual constraint is required, in an age of spiralling consumer debt. Whilst it may appear only distantly related, dealing with the credit and debt culture itself may thus also play an important role in maintaining faith in politics and the public sphere.

# 2 | Politics and Adversarialism

onsumerism is a relatively new challenge to our politics, whilst
adversarialism is part of the British political tradition. But it is
one that is increasingly unsuited to the modern environment.
For example, in the midst of the controversy about US soldiers'
mistreatment of Iraqi prisoners at Abu Ghraib in May 2004,
Conservative leader Michael Howard wrote an article in *The Independent*
suggesting that Tony Blair should be more open with the public about
the concerns he expressed in private to his ally, President Bush.[1] Despite
the restrained nature of these comments, which echoed the feelings of
many in the Labour Party at the time, Howard was immediately and
strongly attacked by government ministers. Speaking on the Today
programme on the day the article was published, the Leader of the
Commons, Peter Hain, suggested that Mr Howard's intervention was
an example of 'shallow opportunism' and indicated 'how unfit he is to
be Prime Minister'. Interviewed later in the programme, Howard
responded in kind by claiming that 'nothing demonstrates more clearly
the arrogance of this government and their contempt for parliamentary
democracy than these charges of opportunism'.

Whilst listeners were no doubt deeply troubled by the revelations of
prisoner mistreatment, and interested in the implications for US-UK
relations of the unfolding situation in Iraq, such rhetoric from both sides
can only have fuelled frustration with the entire political class. Yet this

is just one example of how nuanced conversations in British politics frequently descend into bitter confrontational battles that alienate the electorate.

Our adversarial system has long been dominated by two main political parties, given formal rights at Westminster that are not available to other parties or independents. Although other parties now have well established representation, the mode of exchange remains aggressively tribal. What is supported by one political party is almost invariably opposed by the others. The British public, meanwhile, has become markedly less tribal in its political affiliations. This results from better education and more widely available information about politics. Whilst, in the past, class allegiance or family tradition was a good predictor of voting behaviour, people are now more likely to consider different policies on their merits. The result is a less fixed attachment to parties, and greater likelihood of transferring their votes between elections.

The tribal loyalty of politicians to their own side, and hostility to the proposals of their opponents, is increasingly out of step with this public mood. At its most extreme, this behaviour appears infantile to an increasingly sophisticated electorate. Yet political debates — as facilitated by the media, parliament and most other forums — continue to emphasise the adversarial. This creates the impression that there are only ever two sides to any argument, with each party believing itself to be always right while the others are always wrong. It denies the very essence of politics, which is about negotiation and compromise. There are two rational responses on the part of the public. First, as many do, they can join the politicians in always seeking another set of politicians to blame. Second, being aware that many arguments are complex and multi-faceted, they may feel increasingly alienated by a process that appears constantly to reduce complexity to simplicity. Either way, faith in politics declines.

Only 28 per cent of people say that they are satisfied with politicians, and just 2 per cent are 'very satisfied' with how they do their jobs. This is in stark comparison to the 85-95 per cent who say the same of nurses, doctors and teachers.[2] Yet politicians are the only one of these groups to face an opposition (albeit made up of other politicians) that constantly seeks to question their judgement, criticise their actions and tell the public how and why they are wrong. The public's decision to turn away from the process is hardly surprising.

The structure of British politics traditionally shuts the opposition out of decision making almost completely. Whilst governments can display their commitment through actions, the opposition generally have only words. To achieve recognition their best chance is to criticise the government at every turn, even if the policies pursued are ones they might equally well have adopted themselves. In 2003, for example, the Conservatives sought to profit from Labour divisions and public dissent by opposing the government's policy over university tuition fees. One university Vice Chancellor with strong Conservative Party connections expressed frustration when a frontbench member told him that 'it does not matter whether this is the right policy or the wrong policy', so long as the party could make political capital out of opposing it.[3] Ironically, Conservative opposition on this occasion may have helped to stifle Labour dissent by stoking up tribal loyalties on the government side.[4] Such examples of knee jerk oppositionalism do politics a disservice at two levels. First, by actively seeking to undermine the integrity of the government, they increase general cynicism about politicians. Rather than helping to communicate the idea that politics is difficult and cannot please all the people all the time, they reinforce the belief that the process is constantly failing. Second, a pure oppositionalist stance stifles debate about the complexities of policy, hiding much of the true business of politics from view.

It is easy to find examples of such behaviour by the Conservatives since 1997. But to denounce opposition tactics is not simply to make a partisan point. The system and prevailing culture of national politics drives this behaviour, and it is indulged in by all parties in opposition. This includes the Liberal Democrats (who often seek to undermine both other parties simultaneously), and Labour, before it entered power. Just as today's Conservative front bench attacks this government, Labour politicians prior to 1997 engaged in a daily battle of press releases aimed at undermining virtually all government initiatives. Such criticism goes far beyond the necessary job of pointing out real loopholes or stating principled opposition to particular policy directions. By seeking short term partisan advantage, those engaging in this behaviour corrode the culture of politics and faith in the system itself.

Adversarialism is primarily a cultural issue, but it is encouraged by the structures of British politics. Our institutions shape politicians' incentives and behaviour, and consequently have an important impact on the culture of politics. The most obvious influence is the electoral system for the House of Commons, which tends to exaggerate the vote of the two main parties, under-represent other parties, and deliver single party governments often with large majorities. A change in the electoral system would undoubtedly have a major cultural impact. However, it is not necessarily a precondition to change in the ethos at Westminster. For example, the establishment in the House of Commons in 1979 of select committees to shadow the work of government departments helped develop expertise amongst members, engage MPs in matters of detail, and build allegiances across party lines. Yet these committees continue to involve only a minority of members. The main focus of attention in the Commons remains the adversarial forum of the plenary chamber, and legislation is sent to non specialist 'standing' committees, where opposition MPs are inclined to obstruct progress rather than engage in the more important public duty of seeking to negotiate better law. Indeed, in 2001 a leaked memo from the then Shadow Leader of the House proposed that Conservative members should, rather than doing their best to improve legislation, ensure that bills left the Commons 'imperfectly scrutinised'.[5] Instead of encouraging such behaviour, our political structures should extend the sphere within which constructive negotiation takes place.

Some recent procedural changes at Westminster — for example sending more bills in draft to select committees for consideration — have helped. But more radical reform is needed. For example, establishing permanent legislative committees to take evidence on bills would draw in more members to cross-party work, and help improve the quality of parliament's output. This could help nurture a more constructive culture, as well as better involving outside groups in debate.

Structural reform alone, however, is not enough to deliver change. A shift from an adversarial to a more constructive political culture depends on a conscious effort from politicians. Research, particularly among women voters, has long shown that the 'yah boo' politics which extends from Prime Minister's Questions to the TV studios and beyond is a cultural turn off. The public respects politicians who admit their mistakes and do not claim to know everything. Estelle Morris has reported receiving a round of applause from a studio audience for simply answering 'I don't know'. Rare opposition members seek to adopt a more consensual approach, being willing to agree with government policy on some issues and instead engaging in discussion of detail. Feedback to journalists appears to demonstrate that the public find such an approach refreshing. Yet examples of such behaviour are limited. In certain areas there is a tradition of constructive engagement between the parties — on defence issues particularly it is considered important to minimise divisions in order not to undermine faith in national security and the armed services. But there is no similar sensitivity to the danger of undermining politics itself. This is the challenge that politicians must now rise to. Such change is only likely to be achieved by concerted action, taken by politicians on a cross-party basis. This represents a major cultural challenge, the practicalities of which are further discussed at the end of the pamphlet. Difficult though it may appear, until this is achieved, politics is likely to continue to disappoint.

66

# 3 | Politics and Campaigning

**M**ore frequent elections and new campaign techniques mean that the political campaign has changed in both style and intensity. Campaigning increasingly goes on all year round, and some political communications gurus have suggested that we have reached the age of the 'permanent campaign'.[1] Consequently, the problems attached to campaigning have entered everyday political discourse, rather than being confined to occasional election times.

Campaigning can be divided into two modes: the positive and the negative. Both of these are used by parties to communicate facts about their own policy positions and those of their opponents. Both are potentially useful. However, in their modern forms both approaches may have a detrimental effect on the culture of politics.

Positive campaigning is the more benign of the two. Here, parties seek to communicate their achievements, their values and their plans for future policy. The intention of such messages is to create positive expectations about political outcomes, and inspire hope that politicians can improve the quality of life. These are obviously important messages. But at the same time there is always the danger of creating an impression that politicians can deliver more than is realistic. This, understandably, will feed disappointment.

Overpromising can take many forms. One is for politicians to play down the importance of the external constraints within which they operate—in part due to an unconscious denial of the limits on their own power. These include restrictions placed on UK politicians by the European Union, as well as other international institutions such as the WTO. In addition come the innumerable limitations created by the need to protect business interests—for example, with respect to delivering better working conditions or greater environmental protection. Post-privatisation, politicians even find themselves apologising for poor services that are provided almost entirely by the private sector, such as on the railways. In all these respects there is a reluctance to admit that the state cannot deliver everything. Whilst too many pleas of power-lessness are unlikely to boost respect for politicians, a greater degree of honesty would heighten public understanding of their role. It would also help shift attention to other bodies—such as corporations or the institutions of Europe—which often escape proper accountability.

Overpromising is, in part, linked to the consumer culture, and politi-cians' reluctance to admit the extent to which social change depends on the actions of individuals as responsible citizens. The danger here is that parties are seen as products and politicians, afraid of offending the public, seek to behave as if the 'customer' is always right. This helps explain why John Prescott is held responsible for a broken promise on reducing traffic growth, which in truth could only be brought about by motorists' decisions to change their own behaviour. Government is crit-icised for failing to control obesity, when what is needed to achieve this is a combination of greater corporate responsibility and alteration to individual lifestyles. The changes desired can only be accomplished by a partnership between politicians, the public and other groups. A failure to be frank about this can only fuel disappointment. Remember the difficulty Tony Blair found himself in at one widely broadcast moment of the 2001 general election campaign when collared by an angry voter outside a Birmingham hospital. The Prime Minister sought to placate his critic, who complained of slow progress in reforming the NHS, alleging that 'you are not prepared to pay for it'. Although the midst of an election campaign was hardly the moment for a sudden change of approach, the correct response from Blair might have been to say: 'We, madam, have only the money that taxpayers consent to give us. It is therefore *you* who are not prepared to pay for it!'

Whilst the positive campaign may sometimes feed disappointment, the potential harm it does to politics is mild compared to that of the negative campaign. Some negative campaigning is of course essential to political discourse: just as politicians point out the strengths of their own programmes it is their duty to highlight the weaknesses of their opponents. However, it can also represent adversarialism at its worst, and act to undermine trust.

Though negative campaigning has always been part of our political culture, it has grown in ferocity in recent years. Such campaigns do not just focus on substance, but increasingly on questions of politicians' competence and integrity. In opposition, Labour became masters of this art. Thus the behaviour of some Conservative MPs, including taking payment for tabling parliamentary questions, was mercilessly exploited, allowing allegations of 'sleaze' against the government to stick.[2] In his book documenting Labour's general election campaigns of the 1990s, Philip Gould proudly describes the growing use of negative techniques, explaining how in the run up to 1997 the campaign sought to make Labour appear 'a positive voice in a sea of sleaze and cynicism'.[3] His frank descriptions demonstrate how corrosive this approach can be. Of the party's general 'attacking strategy', he said that 'the strengths are many: it keeps the focus on them; it stops us being the incumbent; it shows [Tony Blair] to be strong; it gives us momentum; ... it means that we are not offering a reason to vote for us. But on balance it is working'.[4] Purely by stirring up cynicism about their opponents, perhaps on the basis of behaviour by a small minority of wayward individuals, the purveyors of the negative campaign can create a relative advantage for their own side. However, this does little to reassure the public that politicians on the whole—even those on the opposing benches—are honest and hardworking, and driven primarily by a sense of public duty rather than a desire for personal gain.

24

Building on the successful campaigns that Labour ran before 1997 using the slogan 'you can't trust the Tories', the Conservatives in opposition have also engaged in increasingly negative techniques. They too have sought to focus on issues of competence and trust, albeit often with little basis in substance. They have not been able to resist exploiting opportunities provided by mischievous press stories, such as so-called 'Cheriegate', to score points against the government. Conservative leader Iain Duncan-Smith clearly saw partisan advantage in his oft-repeated mantra, 'you can't believe a word they say'. This has now been developed by Michael Howard, on the back of the recent Blunkett saga, to suggest that Britain has a 'grubby government'.[5] Piled upon the already negative impressions created about their own party, retaliating by bringing their opponents into equal disrepute may be seen to offer a short term gain. But in the longer term there is a danger of a ratchet effect, with each opposition in turn gradually dragging down the reputation of the political profession further.

Over recent years positive and negative campaigning tactics have reinforced each other. Tony Blair's promise that Labour in government would be 'whiter than white' set unrealistic expectations that were quickly dashed. And Tory attempts to capitalise on any wrongdoing have since exacerbated these negative effects. Both approaches are antithetical to politics.

If the campaign is not to feed disappointment, it too requires cultural change. The continued pursuit by parties of short term political advantage by raising unrealistic expectations about their own powers and seeking to undermine trust in their opponents' integrity, runs the risk of bringing the entire political system into ever greater disrepute. The political profession (and those who report it) will only maintain trust if they set realistic and honest expectations. Campaigns based on more open engagement about policy options, constraints and responsibilities, of individuals as well as the state, seem essential if politicians are to boost public respect.

The more that politicians seek to exploit public disillusionment by telling us that other politicians cannot be trusted, the more the public is likely to take them at their word.[6] With an election on the horizon, the parties face a classic 'prisoner's dilemma' with respect to negative campaigning methods. If one seeks to exploit public mistrust in politics by undermining the other, it may potentially reap electoral benefits. But the ultimate result of such tactics, particularly when pursued by both sides, is that the whole system suffers. Again, the answer lies in a more co-operative and responsible approach, and a cross-party recognition that our culture has to change.

# 4 | Politics and the Media

Modern politics could not function without the media. In a mass democracy, politicians and their supporters cannot communicate directly with voters more than occasionally. The media now provides the framework within which most political communication takes place. A healthy media, and a healthy relationship between the media and politicians, is therefore essential to a healthy democracy.

Problems with the health of this relationship have been the subject of much recent debate. Various journalists have written with passion about the corrosive effect of the media culture on democracy.[1] And these criticisms are not limited to journalists from the left. Peter Oborne, for example, has suggested that the media 'prefer the short-term to the long-term, sentimentality to compassion, simplicity to complexity, the dramatic to the mundane, confrontation to the sensible compromise'. He concludes that 'it is hard to imagine any environment for political decision making that could be more damaging and unhelpful'.[2] Yet this is precisely the environment in which politics is increasingly conducted.

Whilst the media is crucial to politics, it has its own culture and motivations, which can potentially come to be at odds with the ethos of politics. Whilst politics does not constitute a market in the true sense, the media largely does. Competition has always been a major determinant in its culture. However, the increasingly fierce competition caused by today's new technologies and global pressures has some troubling consequences. Decline in market share for newspapers results in cost-cutting and encourages more aggressive journalism and more sensational headlines. Whilst this in itself might not matter much (the trust the public place in newspaper journalists is consistently lower than that in politicians) there are serious problems when this culture spreads. Broadcasting is also becoming more competitive, and newspapers are influential in setting the agenda of the other news media. These factors have a major impact on the way in which politics is communicated, and in turn on how politicians themselves behave. Indeed, the logic of politics has shifted to fit in with that of the media, rather than the other way around. This has left us living in what some have dubbed a 'media democracy'.[3]

There are many concerns about the media, including, for example, issues of privacy and press intrusion. However, what interests us here is the question of how the media culture is antithetical to the culture of politics. This section therefore focuses on just five ways in which this is the case.

The first is the way in which the media feeds adversarialism. It increasingly provides the site where conflicts between political actors are played out. Too often, policy debates are presented as a simplistic argument between two sides — usually government and opposition, but sometimes politicians and their external opponents. Disagreements are particularly celebrated when they occur between members of one party, which leads to caution in expressing opinion for fear of generating 'splits'. All of this generally ensures that the complexity of politics is hidden from view, and that the public is denied the opportunity to engage with the difficult task of balancing the interests involved. Some of the media's more highbrow elements are among the worst offenders on this count, and help to set the tone for other media outlets. In contrast to most everyday conversations, where opinions include shades of grey, interviewees on our top programmes are often carefully vetted to ensure that they will put opposing points of view.

At the time of the fuel protests in 2000 — one of the recent occasions when domestic politics came nearest to collapse — there was little help from the media in presenting the complexities faced by policy makers. Day after day as the crisis developed, Radio 4's Today Programme pitted ministers against the protesters and their sympathisers, who urged them to cut fuel duties to benefit hauliers. Little or no mention was made of the potential environmental benefits which the 'fuel duty escalator' was intended to bring. Then finally, the morning after the Chancellor conceded that the next fuel duty increase would be dropped, ministers on the programme were confronted with representatives of the green lobby, who complained about the consequences for pollution. At a time of national crisis such as this, the responsible reaction from the media would have been to facilitate discussions at the early stages that engaged listeners in the complexity of the issues. Instead, politicians found themselves damned when they did and then damned when they didn't stick to their policy. The ultimate victim in this kind of adversarial showdown is politics itself. Such coverage absolves the public of responsibility, turning citizens into bystanders — consumers, even — rather than participants. The media culture constantly seeks somebody to blame, and it is usually a politician. Far more rarely is it a corporation, an entire industry or even citizens themselves.

The second, and more serious, difficulty is that the adversarial media culture no longer stops at providing a forum for political figures to argue with each other. The media also feeds disengagement by itself adopting an increasingly adversarial attitude towards the whole political class. Professor of Media Studies Stephen Barnett has charted four ages of political journalism, leading from the age of journalistic deference in the 1940s and 1950s to the healthier age of equal engagement in the 1960s and 1970s, followed by the age of journalistic disdain in the 1980s to the age of contempt that he claims we have reached today. As he suggests, the attitude that journalists now display means that 'the notion that politicians are honest, honourable individuals doing their damnedest to make their country a better place does seem faintly odd'.[4]

Media outlets rarely miss an opportunity to imply that politicians are corrupt, hypocritical, or simply inept. To some extent, similar cynicism pertains to all professions, but this is by far the most extreme case. At times, it includes the wilful withholding of information. For example the publication of MPs' expense details in October 2004 was greeted with criticism of the 'scandalous scale of Westminster's gravy train', 'an average of £118,437 in expenses perks' and 'snouts in the trough'.[5] The fact that the vast bulk of 'expenses' comprised the salary costs of staff, plus the rental of office space and other essentials, was omitted from most newspaper reports. And the culture of contempt is not confined to the tabloids alone. Just as the Today Programme sets the standard for adversarialism between politicians, so the Paxman interview — which has created the model for a new generation of interviewers — is the benchmark for demonstrating journalistic scorn towards policy makers. Many senior journalists now present an image of themselves as superior to the second-rate political classes, intimating, as David Walker suggests, that 'they have no power; apparently, they merely frame the questions which "those lying bastards" refuse to answer'.[6]

Politicians themselves have helped fuel the age of contempt, through their growing aggression towards one another. So too have periods of weak opposition, such as the early 1980s and late 1990s, when journalists saw themselves as the only effective force to keep the government of the day in check. And the principle that broadcast journalists should not show bias towards the governing party, whilst being extremely valuable, may also have played a part. One way of not appearing partisan is to criticise each side as severely as the other. Maintaining standards of impartiality whilst not undermining faith in the institution of government itself is a difficult line for broadcasters to tread — but it is clear that there is an urgent need to do so.

Three further factors are more straightforward, but equally important. One is the tendency of the media to report negative rather than positive political stories. Balanced debate requires coverage of the successes as well as the failures of policy. Whilst policy problems, and premonitions of future problems, are widely reported, policies that turn out to work are largely ignored.

At times, journalists themselves have sought to draw attention to such anomalies in reporting. An ironic recent example was found in *The Guardian*. On the day that new crime figures were published, Polly Toynbee's piece in the comment pages was entitled 'What the papers won't say: crime is actually falling'. Sure enough, the front page headline in the same paper the next day proclaimed 'Sharp rise in rape cases overshadows fall in crime rate'. The article focused on the negative aspects of the figures, only grudgingly admitting halfway through that it was probably improved reporting, due to growing confidence in the police, which had resulted in the increased rape figure.[7] With the media providing the public's access to information, and politics so frequently reported to fail, and so rarely to succeed, it seems inevitable that this will feed disappointment.

Meanwhile, though some subjects are reported negatively, or through a simplistic adversarial lens, others get little coverage at all. The focus is generally on announcements that have just been, or are about to be, made, whilst the long term effects of policy have little 'news value'.

Thus, for example, warnings that the national minimum wage would cost a million jobs were widely covered before its introduction. We subsequently heard little about the impact of this important policy change, or indeed the fact that the negative predictions proved to be incorrect. Similarly, coverage of policy making in Europe (particularly in the Parliament) is almost non existent, not least because most newspapers have no Brussels correspondent. In all of these ways the media's basic function to provide information to feed political debate is found seriously wanting.

Finally, though most journalists aspire to inform the public of the truth (even if a partial truth) this is not always the case. The opinion-led reporting of some newspapers may go beyond omitting unwelcome facts. An ex *Daily Mail* journalist appearing on a recent Fabian platform confessed to having been 'constantly under pressure to write things I didn't think were true'. Yet the sanctions against papers publishing incorrect stories are minor, whilst the growing number of stories based on unnamed 'sources' cannot be verified at all.

In short, the growth of mass politics has placed an important duty on the media to facilitate informed political debate. Yet this responsibility is too often overlooked, and is increasingly driven out by market pressures. The media has reported much about declining levels of political trust. But, as David Walker has noted, there is little sign of self-examination with respect to how they contribute to the problem. It is true that not all of the fault lies with the media itself. Politicians, recognising the media's power, altered their mode of communication, leading to 'media management' and 'spin' which, in retrospect, seems to have helped feed cynicism. The culture of modern politics and the press have fuelled each other in unhelpful ways. A return to a culture of constructive engagement, rather than one of either deference or contempt, is necessary if our faith in politics is to be restored.

Yet change is exceptionally difficult to achieve. Journalists guard their independence fiercely, whilst politicians fear the wrath of the media if they dare to criticise it. Compare ministers' readiness to condemn the interference of the unelected House of Lords to their reluctance to criticise the — far less accountable — press. Witness the *The Sun*'s recent chilling response to suggestions of a new privacy law: 'get your tanks off our lawn'. This was coupled with an allegation that 'too many politicians are sad, sordid, pathetic, inadequate wimps with private lives that make ordinary people's stomachs churn'.[8] Individual politicians are left in no doubt about the potential power of the press to drive them out of office. Yet they cannot circumvent the media, and still less should they expect it spontaneously to reform itself. Despite the best efforts of good journalists, the profession as a whole can, in Peter Oborne's words, 'destroy with a pitiless and awesome brutality. But they can rarely create anything new, original and good'.[9]

The answer lies to a large extent in tackling market failures through forms of regulation. The media market is, of course, already regulated, particularly with respect to public service broadcasting. Central to this in the British system is the BBC. The corporation is not only respected worldwide for the quality of its reporting, but is also widely trusted by the British public. It is where citizens go in search of reliable news programmes, with 84 per cent of the public saying they use these for at least 15 minutes per week.[10] A similar percentage say that they trust the BBC's journalists to tell the truth.[11] This makes the BBC a precious resource which should be nurtured, and gives it big responsibilities in maintaining our national political life. Yet the BBC is increasingly subject to competitive pressures, whilst the examples above demonstrate how even its style of political reporting can contribute to the problem. And the events around the Hutton report helped illustrate how fragile public confidence could prove to be. The current charter review process therefore creates both a threat and an opportunity to the BBC. The corporation needs to use this to review and strengthen its role in setting the standard for political reporting, and to bolster high quality factual programming which allows a fair assessment of policy. In return, politicians of all parties must recognise the central role the BBC plays in promoting an engaged politics. It should be free to offer a real alternative, based on quality, rather than being expected to compete in a market. This appears increasingly essential to underpinning the quality of British democracy.

It must also now be time to strengthen press regulation. As Onora O'Neill has suggested, press freedom must be balanced by responsibility, and cannot be expected to extend to the 'freedom to deceive'.[12] The Press Complaints Commission represents one of the last bastions of self-regulation and has proved to be ineffective. A new independent regulator could be given powers to impose meaningful fines on newspapers for publishing untrue stories, and to require corrections of equivalent prominence to the original article. This would not only help stem untruths in the newspapers themselves, but help prevent these infecting the rest of the media.

These changes alone are insufficient, however, to tackle the 'culture of contempt'. A concerted focus needs to be given by responsible journalists, academics and policy makers to rebuilding a healthy relationship between our media and our politics. This is not something that journalists, operating in a competitive market, can deliver on their own. One way forward would be for the government to fund a serious institute, or a standing commission, to oversee the relationship between politics and the media. This government has established an Electoral Commission to promote transparency and good practice by the political parties, and to encourage political engagement, which could offer a model to guide a similar Commission on the Media. Such a body could commission research, promote good journalistic practice, and open the press and broadcasters up to greater scrutiny by the public. It would clearly need to be at arm's length from both the government and the media, but might be overseen by commissioners with respected journalistic and policy experience. This would help make the media more publicly accountable, in a way befitting an industry with such a key role in the democratic process.

# 5 | Politics and Ideology

B ack in 1962, Bernard Crick saw ideology as one of the key threats to political rule. Writing at the height of the Cold War, he argued that politics was the essential alternative to rigid and fully systematic dogmas that could lead to totalitarianism. Yet in later years Crick pointed out that it is not only possible to have too much ideology, but also to have too little. His Fabian pamphlet of 1984 sought to defend politics against dogma on the one hand and 'managerial pragmatism' on the other.[1]

Forty years after Crick's *In Defence of Politics*, it indeed seems that there is too little ideology in politics. Voters have an increasingly confused sense of what the major parties stand for. In theory, each party's policies are underpinned by broad ideological values that enable them to balance priorities between competing demands. Accordingly, when voters make a choice between parties, they decide not between complex packages of policy ideas, but between alternative visions of the future. Yet by 2001 only 29 per cent of voters said they perceived much difference between the parties. This had fallen rapidly, from 55 per cent in 1992, and a high of 84 per cent in 1987.[2] The change appears highly relevant to how people engage with politics, as difference between the parties plays an important part in mobilising citizens. In 2001 the turnout among those perceiving a major difference between the parties was seven per cent higher than among those who believed there was 'not much' difference. Even more strikingly, the level of general satisfaction with the democratic system was 22 per cent higher among the former group.[3]

Twentieth-century British politics was not strongly ideological, arguably being more class-based than value-based. The Labour Party itself was founded primarily as a vehicle for representation of the working class, and only later adopted a socialist constitution. The widening of the franchise, however, forced all parties to compete for the votes of this group in order to survive. Although Labour was recognised as their 'natural choice', the Tories always managed to win substantial portions of the working class vote. In terms of policy positions there was much common ground between the parties, as a result of both external constraints and competition for votes. They frequently 'stole each other's clothes', and the immediate post-war period in particular was famous for the degree of consensus between the two main parties over broad policy direction.[4] Nonetheless, the rhetoric and culture of the two main parties throughout this time remained distinct, even when their approach to the substance of policy was similar. This helped ensure that tribal loyalties survived.

It is generally accepted that loyalty to parties has fallen as a result of the weakening of class identities. The decline of unionised heavy industry, in particular, broke up Labour's traditional support base, whilst growing wealth and rising aspirations saw more 'natural' Labour supporters drift to the Conservatives. In addition, improved standards of education and the growth of the mass media over the post-war period created an electorate prepared to break with family or class traditions and make up its own mind about policy. The creation of 'New Labour' was in large part a reaction to these trends.

From 1994 onwards, Tony Blair sought to make a virtue of rejecting traditional ideology, declaring Labour to be 'neither old left nor new right'. This was a highly successful electoral strategy, addressing the persistent fears that many voters had of the party. But the rejection of the notion of two established political poles (however fictional), has

eroded already weakened loyalties further still. This has been exacerbated by the fact that since this time Labour's values have often not been
explicit—meaning that new loyalties have not been established to
replace the old. Most recently, the government has claimed to be driven
by 'delivery' and 'what works', rather than by a distinct vision of the
better society. Whilst the old rhetoric that emphasised continuity with
tradition provided an apparent ideological anchor, this new environment threatens to leave many voters disorientated and confused.

Some of the techniques of modern political communications have fed
these trends. New methods of polling and the use of focus groups have
made it possible for politicians to respond to the views of the electorate
in ever more sophisticated ways. Yet whilst these methods are undoubtedly valuable in making politicians more responsive, they also have
their limitations. If focus groups become the means of setting policy,
what results is unlikely to be coherent or to take account of the conflicts
central to politics. As David Marquand remarks, 'politics is a process
not of registering preferences but of changing them'.[5] The Thatcher
governments successfully communicated values to the electorate that
changed (for good or ill) the way people thought and behaved. This
shift in public values, rather than any single policy, was arguably the
greatest legacy of Thatcherism. If Labour is to have a lasting impact, an
equivalent shift in values needs to be achieved.

Almost four decades ago Otto Kirchheimer predicted the rise of 'catch
all' parties, which would be less ideological and would instead aim to
appeal to a wide electorate, being flexible enough to shift their positions
in response to the public mood. In Britain this pull to the centre ground
may have been accelerated, given the parties' need to appeal to a few
median voters in target seats. But Kirchheimer was sceptical about
where such developments would lead, noting that 'the catch-all party
cannot be much more rational than its nominal master, the individual
voter.' Over time, 'the voters may, by their shifting moods and their
apathy, transform the sensitive instrument of the catch-all party into
something too blunt to serve as link with the functional powerholders

of society'.[6] He thus predicted that parties which respond only to public opinion would lose their ideological coherence and, ironically, their ability to retain voters' loyalty. This could describe the point we have now reached. It again demonstrates how the short term interests of each party may be in conflict with that party's long term interests, and with the interests of the political system as a whole.

It may seem odd to suggest that British politics has become more adversarial at the same time that it has become less ideologically divided. But in fact this pattern has a peculiar logic. As the parties have become more similar in both style and substance, they have needed to demonstrate publicly their differences in other ways. This is seen both in the workings of parliament and in politics at large. In parliament, whips need to try harder to stir up tribal loyalties and persuade members to vote for policies that might equally have been proposed by the opposition. The vote on introducing variable university top-up fees was a recent case in point. Outside parliament, parties seek to rely on voters' vestigial tribal sentiments but these, as we have seen, are on the decline. This may leave no choice but to engage in opportunistic and personality-driven attacks, which simply undermine faith in the system.

All of this suggests that to win voters' loyalty, parties need to communicate their values and offer distinct visions of the future, between which choices can be made. In the absence of old class loyalties, these are the only stable poles around which voters can be asked to navigate. This is not to call for a return to the sharp ideological divisions that (unusually) defined British politics in the early 1980s. Rather, the challenge is for the parties to identify and articulate with subtlety what divides left and right in a post cold-war world. Under the consumer model of politics offered by the catch-all party—where voters shop around for competent managers—the electorate seems destined to become increasingly disappointed. Only if values are explicit can voters decide which chime most closely with their own, and thus broadly which side they are on.

It is the ability to offer these big choices that differentiates politics from consumerism, and encourages citizens to engage in a distinct way. Politics enables moral choices, rather than market choices, to be taken by society on a collective basis. And there are many signs that voters are seeking such alternatives. The wave of optimism which accompanied Labour's victory in 1997 appeared to show the British public's desire for a new direction, based on a more caring and inclusive politics. Labour in opposition had become increasingly nervous about openly stating its beliefs for fear of exposing internal dissent or finding itself in conflict with the public mood. Yet many of its policies in government have been distinctly progressive, from significant redistribution of wealth through the tax and benefits system to investment in public services, from increased overseas aid to improved workers' rights or liberal attitudes to sexuality. These policies have generally won public support, although the values underlying them have rarely been articulated. An approach which presented a more coherent vision based on centre-left values thus has significant potential to capture voters' attention and support.

But a more value-based approach also brings other important benefits. First, it may make voters more tolerant of political leaders. As Michael Jacobs put it in 2002, ideology gives people a 'reason to believe'.[7] If voters are convinced of leaders' intentions they are more likely to accept slow progress, so long as the overall direction of travel is clear. Rather than measuring whether governments are moving towards public service 'targets', they can be judged by whether they are adhering to their values. Politicians can express more honesty about the constraints within which they operate if at the same time they clearly articulate their objectives, and are seen to be faithful to them. Second, clear values provide reasons for people to join and work for a party. Values provide an essential 'glue' that binds parties together. Their absence from debate may help explain parties' current decline.

Moving to a more value-based politics is no easy matter, although the potential benefits may be great. The British parties are necessarily broad churches, accommodating diverse strands of opinion. Nonetheless, it should be possible for the left to put down markers in terms of objectives that its opponents would find it difficult to support. Whilst articulating these might alienate some voters it would give many others reason to believe. It would also put the opposition onto the defensive, requiring them to state whether they agreed with the sentiments proposed, and to present alternatives of their own. This potentially moves the entire political ground towards the left.

A more ideological politics, however, also requires new mechanisms within the parties. Groups such as Compass and New Wave Labour have recently been formed by Labour members keen to explore the articulation and application of centre-left values in the twenty-first century.[8] But such matters should properly be central to the discussions within the party itself. Despite Labour's traditional internal structures for making policy, there is no forum for debating the more fundamental framework of values that should guide policy, and how that framework should evolve in a changing world. The last time such issues were examined was during the revision of Clause IV, now a decade ago. Even then, with Labour nervous after 16 years in opposition, the exercise was far less open than it might otherwise have been.

Richard Brooks has recently suggested in the *Fabian Review* that a decade is long enough to wait for another review of the party's values.[9] This is certainly true. There is not only a need to review how the left's traditional values of liberty, equality and fraternity fit in the modern world, but also how fresh challenges — such as those created by new technologies and environmental threats — can be met. Yet the solution should not be another one-off event that heightens sensitivities about party unity, but an ongoing debate. Public intellectuals, and the Fabian Society itself, have an important role to play in providing the terms and the forum for this debate. But the party's own structures should also facilitate it.

The Partnership in Power arrangements for debating Labour's policy are currently under review, amid tensions (as old as the party itself) about the appropriate role of party members and affiliates in determining programmes for implementation by Labour governments. One appropriate outcome of these discussions would be the establishment of a forum where party values could regularly be debated. This might, for example, comprise a day at each year's annual conference where core values, and the priorities between them, were discussed. This would capture the imagination of those in the party, and help communicate Labour's developing ideas to the wider world. But it would also help underpin action for Labour in government, and could defuse some of the traditional tensions about policy making. Whilst it may be impractical for the extra-parliamentary party to determine all of a Labour government's policies in detail, the party should have a core role in helping to define political direction, and a forum within which this is regularly debated.

# 6 | Politics and Political Parties

If there is one thing harder than finding someone who will defend
politics it is finding anyone who will defend the political parties. In
debates about political disengagement, parties are often seen as
central to the problem. The number of people who say that they are very
strong supporters of one or other of the parties has consistently
declined, from 45 per cent in 1964 to seven per cent in 2003.[1] Meanwhile,
party membership continues to fall, and those who are members of
parties, or donate money to them, are treated with increasing suspicion.

Yet political parties remain an essential feature of a mass democracy.
Not only is their presence inevitable, in order to draw up policy
programmes, offer choices to voters and provide organisation in parliament; it is also highly desirable. For it is within parties that much of the
vital business of politics, as defined in this pamphlet, goes on. In
devising programmes across the full range of policies—from health to
education, business regulation to community policing—the mainstream
parties must balance competing interests, whilst seeking to adhere to
their own principles and devising costed and affordable proposals.
Testing these at elections, and through scrutiny by the media, opposition parties and other groups, allows parties to be held to account.
Without them, politics would be just a mass of uncoordinated individuals building coalitions on an issue-by-issue basis and fighting for electoral support on the basis of personal popularity. The result would not

only be inefficient, it would also offer little in terms of accountability. And it would be unlikely to result in coherent policy or fair distribution of resources. Refreshingly, despite their general lack of enthusiasm, the voters do appear to recognise this. In 1997, over three quarters agreed that political parties were necessary for the democratic system.[2]

It has become fashionable to talk of the decline of political parties in the same breath as the growth of single issue politics. Yet whilst single issue groups may form an indispensable part of building coherent policy, they can never manage this by themselves. By definition they value one objective above all others – with a bewildering range of groups supporting priorities as diverse as greater childcare provision, more road building, higher pensions or more support for cancer research. Politicians must adjudicate between these claims, and apply judgement to ensure that policy is not simply driven by whoever shouts loudest. This is not always an easy task. As one ex-minister has written, 'I would have benefited from a more grown up dialogue between those advocating the different [policy options] rather than simplistic and purist opposition to them all'.[3] Yet this is generally the reality, as the role of interest groups is to maintain pressure on politicians on behalf of their cause, and their cause alone. Though a pluralism of such groups has merits, it also appeals to the consumer culture in ways that can undermine the political ethos. In seeking members and financial support, interest groups tend to focus on blaming politicians, and asking them to act, rather than encouraging campaigns to get individuals and other groups to change. As one expert has put it, pressure group activity can lead to 'a vicious circle of enhanced demands for action, inadequate resources to make a response and increased public dissatisfaction'.[4] Yet if politicians and parties are weakened, rule by single issue groups is by no means a preferable alternative. Rather, this would be a recipe for inequity and governance by vested interest, with moneyed interests always likely to win out.

One role of broad programmatic parties is to present a framework of general values within which individual demands can be considered. It has already been argued that a healthy politics would make these values more visible to voters and party members alike. If the parties do not play this role, no other groups can effectively do so. The democratic principle operating inside parties then provides an additional layer of accountability for politicians, who are required (even minimally) to seek support from members for policy platforms, and adhere to them. Though this internal party democracy is often criticised, it compares well to the organisation of most pressure groups, where the equivalent structures are often non-existent. Thus whilst Greenpeace and Friends of the Earth may between them have more members than the political parties, their members cannot vote to decide who should lead the organisation or what policy positions it should adopt. Their role is primarily to receive briefings and be asked to contribute money and participate in campaigns (largely targeted at politicians). Whilst the energy put into pressure groups is impressive, they do not offer a model of political accountability.

Given this vital importance of parties as the debating ground for policies and politics, it is surprising that so little is heard in their defence. And it is particularly surprising that elected politicians themselves, all of whom have reached office by rising through party ranks, are so silent on this matter. Politicians of course spend much of their time working in their own parties, particularly at election time, and keeping in touch with local members and campaigns. But as faith in the parties has slumped, so politicians – ever sensitive to public opinion – have tended to be increasingly apologetic about their role. If politicians themselves will not defend parties' importance *per se* to the democratic system, it is difficult to see who else will. This can only deepen the crisis of trust.

Mainstream politicians at times contribute to the problem, reinforcing the belief that parties are fundamentally problematic. Tighter rules now apply in public appointments against candidates who are members of, or donors to, political parties. One rather extraordinary example of this was seen in 2000, when the Electoral Commission was created to regulate the parties themselves, and to encourage participation in politics.

The legislation creating this key organisation states that none of its five commissioners may be a member of a political party, and none may have been active in a party, or have made a major party donation, for at least 10 years.[5] The same rules on party activism—far more onerous than those applied even to the most senior civil servants—were, even more exceptionally, also extended to all of the Commission's staff. Thus the body overseeing the parties, and regulating the elections in which they participate, has no up-to-date internal expertise about the way that the parties work. This potentially disadvantages the Commission in its important duties, including its efforts to maximise political participation. The absurdity of this situation further strengthens the impression that parties are unsavoury organisations best kept in their place by those unsullied by their association.

The government has responded to concerns about citizen participation in part through plans for new bodies such as foundation hospitals and New Deal for Community boards. Advocates of the 'social capital' theory argue that public involvement in community decision-making forums like these, as well as being beneficial in itself, can lead to greater engagement in the political process. However, government initiatives have often, intentionally or unintentionally, cut out the political parties. For example, the expectation is that local elected representatives on New Deal for Community boards will not stand under a party banner. Moves such as these can help reinforce the view that parties are outdated, unrepresentative and out of touch. But there is a danger that this approach further distances the public from the parties. It also seems probable that such approaches simply won't work. Once in office, members will tend to form groups that coalesce around particular programmes. And it is difficult to win elections on a wide franchise without institutional backing. It is for these reasons that political parties formed in the first place.

In fact, parties or party-like organisations are already effectively contesting local elections to the new bodies. For example, community representatives on the EC1 New Deal in London have been formally backed by (though not officially representing) the Independent Working Class Association—a breakaway left group which has run candidates in local elections and for London Mayor. The mainstream parties, meanwhile, do not participate. The phenomenon of the 'Independent Kidderminster Hospital and Health Concern' group is well known, having secured the victory of Richard Taylor MP in 2001. Initially a single issue group, the organisation was forced to address the full range of policy issues once it won control of Wyre Forest District Council in 2002. The removal of established parties from local elected bodies, therefore, does not guarantee party-free elections, but simply spawns new parties in opposition to the old. But these will often be single issue parties, whose rise would equate to government by single issue groups. Worse still, we are seeing the threat from 'anti politics' parties, which feed on public dissatisfaction and take extremist positions that undermine the basis of politics itself. Established politicians will not regain trust by trying to circumvent or distance themselves from the mainstream parties. Instead they need to celebrate and seek to revive them. The defence of political parties by politicians is an essential first step in improving faith in the political system.

In recent years various factors have conspired to weaken the parties as organisations. Their traditional role in communicating with the electorate has been largely usurped by the media, while incentives to join have diminished given the numerous other leisure options on offer. Parties have become more dependent on paid workers, major donors and state support (for example through payment to parliamentary staff). Meanwhile, links between members and local communities have tended to decline. For a period it became fashionable to question the value of party members and local parties, believing that leaders could rely entirely on national messages delivered through the media and a central party machine in the American presidential style.[6] But the problems with this model have become increasingly clear. The shortcomings of the media environment have already been described, whilst vibrant local campaigns have been shown to have an impact on electoral outcomes which continues to be significant.[7] The mutual dependence between party leaders and local members is thus inescapable.

Politicians need to acknowledge that the parties are a resource, a source of ideas and energy, and an important intermediary between elected representatives and the public. They not only provide bodies at election time, but also facilitate communication with the public, and are needed to provide tomorrow's political leaders. New democratic arrangements established by government should therefore aim to renew the parties, and include their members, rather than excluding them. Supporting the parties does not mean, as some have proposed, providing increased state funding for party machines, as this may simply further reduce links to activists and local communities. But tax relief on small donations to parties, as currently applies to charities, would help underline their importance to the democratic system. It would also encourage improved links between parties and their supporters.

These changes alone will not be enough, unless the parties also reform themselves. If political parties are to be seen as worth joining by those who are passionate about political issues, they must provide a real site of negotiation with political leaders. Labour's Partnership in Power reforms promised to build just such an open and mature relationship between party leaders and members. But although this system increased dialogue to some extent it has ultimately generated disappointment.[8] It suffered from insufficient resources, with the funding priority always being national campaigns at election time rather than internal party development. It also perpetuated unrealistic expectations, suggesting that Labour members would actually determine the policies of Labour in government. But most damagingly, the system was dogged by a lack of trust on both sides, with leaders insufficiently willing to see members as a genuine source of inspiration and ideas, and many members suspicious of leaders' motives.

Reform of Labour's policy making machinery is now promised, and in the previous chapter it was suggested that this should include the facility to debate the values guiding policy, as well as the detail of policies themselves. More transparency is also needed within the system — for example, local parties should be able to view each others' submissions via the Party's website. But any such reforms will fail unless there is also a cultural change, so that members are convinced that their contributions are valued and that leaders genuinely want to listen.

Thus a key part of ending the disappointment is a re-engagement not only between the voters and the politicians, but between the politicians and the parties that sustain them. This requires honesty by leaders about the constraints of office, and real consultation with parties, as well as the public, about difficult decisions. The potential prize — a better engagement between the parties and the voters — is great.

# Conclusion
# Building a New Culture of Politics

This pamphlet has suggested that there is one central factor at the heart of our current democratic difficulties: the failure by participants throughout the system to recall the purpose and essential nature of politics itself. As Bernard Crick tells us, politics is 'a sociological activity which has the anthropological function of preserving a community grown too complicated for either tradition alone or pure arbitrary rule to preserve it without the undue use of coercion'.[1] It is inevitably an imperfect process. Politics does not allow everyone to get what they want. It is messy and complex, and involves difficult negotiation and compromise. But it is the only peaceful and fair way of tackling the big questions that face us as a society. It should give us cause not for despair, but for celebration. Everything from our lack of civil unrest to the fact that our bins get emptied demonstrates the ability of politics to do its job. Indeed, it is this very success that has allowed many people to fall into complacency, or even political apathy. Some have suggested that this is simply the natural consequence of successful democracy, and should not give us cause for panic. But such a situation holds dangers, and the potential seeds of instability. The impression that politics is merely 'what politicians do' – and that they fail us much of the time – has become corrosive. Without public participation, the legitimacy of our institutions is brought into doubt. A slide into ever greater disappointment with the political system could ultimately prove impossible to reverse.

The environment in which politics exists has changed radically since mass democracy first emerged in Britain a century and more ago. We are a wealthier, better educated and more complex society, and have benefited from great technological advances. Modern politics has helped bring about these changes, but has failed to respond to them adequately. The adjustments that have been made, rather than reviving politics, seem in many ways to be accelerating its decline. Mass consumerism and new methods of political communication have contributed to the perception that politics is a kind of marketplace where politicians 'deliver' in return for individual voters' support. Added to this, the adversarial traditions of British politics have led to an aggressive environment where public debate often overlooks the big questions that politics exists to address, and the competing visions of the future that only it can help us negotiate. The essential nature of politics, requiring compromise and negotiation, and a partnership between citizens and politicians, is hidden from view. Meanwhile, unrealistic expectations are set, and negative campaigns actively seek to undermine trust. And the media's failure to impart the information needed for educated debate leaves politics struggling to survive in an increasingly hostile environment. All of this runs counter to the culture needed to nurture political rule. As Roy Hattersley has suggested, 'the public have lost faith in politicians because many politicians have lost faith in politics'.[2]

We now face a choice. The road on which we are travelling leads at worst to an ever more consumer-oriented politics, where popularity depends on personality and managerial competence, and catch-all parties prevail, unanchored in any clear or distinct sets of values. Here campaigns are ever more aggressive and personal, targeted at winning the votes of a shrinking pool of engaged citizens. If trust in the established parties continues to decline this seems likely to spawn a growth in single issue or anti-politics parties, which cannot adequately resolve the big questions facing society. Instead they will simply contribute to a downward spiral of political trust.

The alternative road leads in a more positive direction, but travelling there requires determined intervention, and some extremely challenging cultural changes. Here we reap the benefits of a better educated electorate and communication methods to create a more engaged politics that allows citizens collectively to consider the big choices facing society. In this model, politicians seek a more honest dialogue with the electorate, admitting constraints, debating the best use of resources and explaining frankly when social change is dependent on changes to individual citizens' behaviour. Real choices are offered on the basis of alternative visions of how society ought to develop, and solutions are negotiated openly according to the views that are expressed. Achieving such a shift requires major changes in behaviour, as indicated below, particularly by politicians and the media. It may therefore appear a somewhat utopian ideal. However, if the alternative is a continuing decline in trust and engagement, this is surely the route we must take.

It is obviously more appealing to look for a quick fix solution to the problem of political disengagement. Hence the proposals to address our problems by extending postal voting, creating an elected replacement for the House of Lords, drafting a written constitution or even restricting the last vestiges of the royal prerogative. Compared to the challenges of cultural change, such solutions are tangible, practical, and indeed seem appealing. Yet there is little evidence that they will bring the solution we seek. For example, levels of political trust in Scotland remain low, despite politicians' response to popular demands for a new Scottish Parliament.[3] The Parliament is elected by a proportional system (another favoured goal of reformers), but has nonetheless adopted much of the adversarialism of the modern British system, and has a similarly bad relationship with the press. More recently, the attempt to create an elected regional assembly in the north east of England was rejected by voters, after the anti-devolution campaign exploited cynicism about politicians, arguing that there was no need to create yet

51

more of them. Structural change without a meaningful commitment to a change of culture will simply perpetuate our current difficulties, or may even create new disappointments.

The purpose of this pamphlet was not simply to lament the problem, but to propose practical ways of resolving it. A number of recommendations were made in earlier sections, and these are summarised below. Those in the first list fall into the more tangible category, and are potentially the more attractive. Each is intended to encourage the kind of cultural change needed to build a new more honest and engaged politics. Nonetheless these proposals on their own are unlikely to be enough. Suggestions for a more concerted change to political culture are therefore given afterwards.

•       A new relationship between citizens and politicians cannot be achieved unless the way it is mediated is improved. Changes to the relationship between the media and politics must be encouraged by celebrating good journalism, rather than simply trying to clamp down on the bad. It is proposed that a new national institute or Commission on the Media be established, to conduct research, highlight good practice and provide for better public scrutiny of media outlets themselves. This level of investment, and of transparency, is appropriate for an industry with such a central role in the political process.

•       Trust in the broadcast media must be maintained, and indeed enhanced. The BBC's charter review offers an opportunity to protect the quality of political reporting of one of the most respected broadcasters in the world. The BBC has a unique role in setting the tone for political reporting, and should not see its standards driven down by competitive pressures. It must maintain its independence, but also recognise its responsibility to improve the standards of political information and debate. It must contribute to accountability without stumbling into the kind of aggressive and negative reporting that undermines the whole political profession.

•      Although the broadcast media is the most important and trusted source of news, the print media, struggling for survival in an increasingly competitive market, greatly influences its behaviour. Press freedom is clearly vital to democracy, but so too is responsible reporting. Greater regulation now appears essential to maintain standards. Voluntarism is no longer enough, and it is proposed that a statutory Press Complaints Commission is created, with meaningful powers.

•      It will be difficult to strengthen politics if it becomes increasingly isolated within a rampant consumer culture and creeping market ethos. Whilst ongoing public service reform to improve standards for users is therefore essential, this must always seek to maintain and celebrate the distinctive public service ethos. The language of efficiency in public service must not parrot that of the market, but be based on a distinct citizen relationship. Furthermore, users will find it difficult to recognise the necessary limits on public services whilst the consumer culture continues to tell them that there are no limits on their own purchasing power. This requires that the culture of excessive credit and debt is tackled, and emphasis placed on self-fulfilment outside the market.

•      Broad programmatic political parties play an essential role in democracy, and their decline is potentially dangerous for politics. Government policy should always seek to support the continued health of the parties, and not sink into sidelining them or stigmatising those who choose to join them. Relationships between parties and their members and supporters could be strengthened through introducing tax relief on small political donations. This would also help demonstrate that parties are just as valuable to society as charities, which are currently in receipt of such relief.

• The parties themselves must do far more, both locally and nationally, to connect with the electorate in meaningful ways. They should be a site of honest engagement between leaders and members, in order that the latter are motivated and feel that they have influence. Only in this way will people feel that parties are worth joining and contributing to. For Labour, the review of Partnership in Power offers an opportunity to start building these arrangements. As well as addressing the existing policy making process, it is suggested that there should be regular opportunities to discuss the values that underlie policy. Such a reform would provide a greater sense of purpose within the party, and make explicit the alternative visions between which voters are asked to choose.

• Further action is necessary to break down the corrosive adversarial culture of modern politics, particularly at Westminster. For example, changes to the committee system of the House of Commons to draw more members into select committee work and to create permanent legislative committees would encourage cross-party collaboration, whilst also improving the quality of parliamentary outputs.

We should not be deceived into thinking that these proposals alone, significant though they are, will boost citizens' engagement. If the culture of politics is the problem it is changes to culture that must hold the solutions. It has been argued that the behaviour of politicians has inadvertently done much to fuel the current disengagement. Only a conscious change in this behaviour will ultimately result in faith in the political profession being enhanced. This is not to downplay the many initiatives that are being taken by individual politicians locally to connect with voters in new and innovative ways. But the danger is that these efforts are drowned out by the so-called 'air war' of national campaigning and media debate that filters through to politics on the doorstep.

In large part the problems have resulted from natural competition in the political system, whereby individual parties' pursuit of short-term gain has—over time—inflicted damage on the system as a whole. Competitive behaviour by political parties is a central requirement of a functioning democracy and it would be absurd and dangerous to attempt to end it. But healthy competition on substantive policy issues, and scrutiny that keeps government accountable, need not be in conflict with respect for the integrity of politics. Without such an approach, public perceptions of the worth of the process are only likely to decline. The difficult part of achieving change is for politicians to put aside their obvious differences, in order to defend the culture of political rule itself. This means taking responsibility, through concerted cross-party efforts, for promoting behaviour that supports rather than undermines its ethos.

## A new political charter

The final concrete proposal is therefore that politicians be encouraged to sign up to a basic 10-point charter of behaviour essential to defend politics against declining participation and falling levels of trust. This is as follows:

• Frankness about the purpose of politics. Admitting that politics is hard, that tough choices have to be made, and that not everyone can win all the time. Celebrating the centrality of debate, negotiation and compromise.

• Carving out a distinct political sphere. Making clear that parties and politicians are not products in a market, that politics is governed by different rules, and that citizenship can fulfil human aspirations that consumerism cannot.

•  Offering political leadership. Acknowledging that, whilst politicians must of course be responsive to voters, it is also their role to spell out the big choices facing society.

•  Making values explicit. Explaining the vision that underlies policy and how this underpins particular decisions. Resisting the 'catch-all' party by admitting that action is guided by values, and spelling out what these values are.

•  Honesty about constraints, including the financial constraints within which policy decisions are taken, and the responsibilities of others, including citizens, to play a part in bringing about change.

•  Being prepared to show fallibility. Admitting mistakes, explaining changes of policy and stating when an answer is unknown or impossible to give.

•  Rejecting opposition for opposition's sake. Being prepared to state when politicians from other parties are right. Not attacking opponents unless an alternative course of action is clear and achievable, and not getting trapped by journalists into knee jerk opposition.

•  Responsible campaigning. Avoiding both exaggerated promises and corrosive attacks on the opposition.

•  Defending political parties. Not forgetting how all current politicians arrived in office, and being explicit about how parties' continued health is essential to the system.

•  Not exploiting lack of voter trust. Perhaps most important of all, not seeking short term gain from the current culture of disengagement. Respecting the integrity of opponents and resisting allegations of dishonesty or corruption except in the rare and isolated circumstances where these are justified. Instead promoting politicians—including those of opposing parties—as hardworking individuals driven by a sense of duty and belief in building a better society.

Although the behaviour of politicians is central to the culture of politics, they are not alone in displaying methods that damage public trust. In particular, as already noted, it will be impossible to achieve major change without a different media culture. The media must in large part provide the forums where a more engaged politics can take place. The three specific reforms above are designed as first steps to help bring this about. But delivering change also depends on those at the heart of the media taking responsibility and showing the determination to promote, rather than further damage, honest and engaged politics. Just as a new pact is necessary from politicians, so good journalists must also work collectively to restore faith in the political process (and indeed in their own profession). We need a media that promotes honesty in reporting, covers good as well as bad political news, presents the complexity of arguments rather than providing stories in simplistic black and white, assumes good faith by politicians unless there is clear evidence to the contrary and expresses scepticism rather than cynicism when holding politicians to account.

Finally, however, it is not simply the responsibility of the traditional political elite to change the perception of politics. This responsibility is also shared by individuals and groups outside. It has been suggested that interest groups, for example, heighten unrealistic expectations of politicians when they continue to make ever greater demands on them rather than also drawing attention to the responsibilities of citizens and other groups. Citizens too have grown accustomed to sitting and waiting for politicians to act, rather than reflecting on what they can usefully do to change their own behaviour and that of those around them. All of us — not just the politicians — therefore have a responsibility to recognise the constraints on politics and to create an environment within which it can effectively work.

In reflecting on the future it is important to remember that mass democratic politics is young, even in Britain. Only in the last 60 years has a stable period of mass politics in peacetime occurred. Democracy communicated through the modern mass media is even younger than that. Whilst it is therefore easy to be complacent about the survival of healthy democratic politics, this in fact is far from guaranteed. This pamphlet has argued that Britain has yet to make an effective transition to a mass democracy populated by an educated and wealthy electorate. But it is essential that we now manage this transition. The growing assertiveness of both public and press in the modern political age has brought the politics of deference to an end. This is no bad thing. But it now needs to be replaced by a new politics, not of disrespect and disappointment but of informed engagement. Politicians, the media, campaign groups and we ourselves, as citizens, have an essential role in helping to construct it.

# Notes

## Introduction: Must Politics Disappoint?

1. Martin Wattenburg, 'The Decline of Party Mobilisation' and R.J. Dalton, 'The Decline of Party Identifications', in R.J. Dalton and M.P. Wattenburg (eds.), *Parties without Partisans: Political Change in Advanced Industrial Democracies* (Oxford: Oxford University Press, 2000).
2. Electoral Commission, *An Audit of Political Engagement* (March 2004). 26 per cent said they trusted politicians 'a fair amount', whilst 51 per cent trusted them 'not very much' and 19 per cent 'not at all'.
3. *An Audit of Political Engagement*, p.46.
4. Bernard Crick, *In Defence of Politics* (London: Continuum, 2000), p.21.
5. *Ibid*, p.26.
6. *Ibid*, pp.15, 141.

## Chapter One: Politics and Consumerism

1. See for example Colin Crouch, *Commercialisation or Citizenship: Education Policy and the Future of Public Services* (London: Fabian Society, 2003); Roger Levett, *A Better Choice of Choice: Quality of Life, Consumption and Economic Growth* (London: Fabian Society, 2003); Colin Leys, *Market Driven Politics* (London: Verso, 2001). In addition, Catherine Needham's *Citizen-consumers: New Labour's Marketplace Democracy* (Catalyst, 2003) touches on some of the issues discussed in this section.
2. David Marquand, *Decline of the Public* (Cambridge: Polity, 2004).
3. Government Strategy Unit paper by David Halpern and Clive Bates, *Personal responsibility and changing behaviour: the state of knowledge and the implications for public policy* (London: Cabinet Office, 2004).
4. Roger Levett, *A Better Choice of Choice: Quality of Life, Consumption and Economic Growth* (London: Fabian Society, 2003).
5. MORI data. The 'Just Listening' exercise carried out in 2004 by a group of Labour MPs and published by the Fabian Society also found that members of the public welcomed honesty and appreciated that solving many policy problems requires a combination of political action

and individuals taking responsibility for their behaviour.

6. The example of participatory budgeting in Brazil has been highlighted by Archon Fung and Eric Olin Wright in *Deepening Democracy: Institutional Innovations in Empowered Participatory Governance* (London: Verso, 2003) and a similar approach proposed for the UK by Angela Eagle, *A Deeper Democracy* (London: Catalyst, 2003).

## Chapter Two: Politics and Adversarialism

1. 'Tony Blair must be more honest over Iraq', 20 May 2004. See http://argument.independent.co.uk/commentators/story.jsp?story =522950. Subsequent debates may be found at http://www.bbc.co.uk/radio4/today/listenagain/zthursday_20040520.sht ml

2. Mori survey, March 2004. See http://www.mori.com/polls/2004/bma.shtml.

3. Patrick Wintour, 'University chief hits at Tories over fees', *The Guardian*, 12 December 2003.

4. One Conservative MP defied the whip at the bill's second reading to vote with the government and two abstained. Had more rebelled, this would have fed the line by Labour opponents that fees were fundamentally a 'Tory' policy. As it was, Labour whips were able to pressurise people by saying that a vote against the bill was a vote for the Tories.

5. See House of Commons Hansard, 19 Mar 2002, Column 168.

## Chapter Three: Politics and Campaigning

1. N.J. Ornstein and T.E. Mann (eds.), *The Permanent Campaign and its Future* (Washington: The AEI Press, 2001).

2. See Oonagh Gay and Patricia Leopold (eds.), *Conduct Unbecoming: The Regulation of Parliamentary Behaviour* (London: Politico's, 2004).

3. Philip Gould, *The Unfinished Revolution* (London: Little, Brown, 1998), p.350.

4. *Ibid*, p.381.

5. Specifically, Howard made the headlines on 21 December 2004 by claiming this was 'a grubby government low on integrity, light on honesty, and lacking in all humility'. See

http://www.tory.org.uk/tile.do?def=news.story.page&obj_id=118257.
This was despite the fact that Howard himself faced allegations that he
had 'fast tracked' a passport for Spectator journalist Petronella Wyatt
when he was Home Secretary.
6. Most recently we have even seen the extraordinary phenomenon of a
government presiding over falling crime figures seeking to shore up its
popularity by promising to protect the public from the perceived
heightened threat of crime.

## Chapter Four: Politics and the Media

1. See John Lloyd, *What the Media are Doing to Our Politics* (London:
Constable and Robinson, 2004); Martin Kettle, 'The threat to the media
is real: it comes from within' and 'Who am I to tell you what to think
about politics', *The Guardian*, 3 February and 22 June 2004; Polly
Toynbee, 'Labour should ignore the media, not appease them', *The
Guardian*, 22 December 2004; David Walker and Nicholas Jones,
*Invisible Political Actors: The Press as Agents of Anti-politics* (London:
New Politics Network, 2004).
2. Peter Oborne and Simon Walters, *Alastair Campbell* (London: Aurum,
2004), p.108.
3. Thomas Meyer and Lew Hinchman, *Media Democracy: How the
Media Colonize Politics* (Cambridge: Polity, 2002).
4. Stephen Barnett, 'Will a Crisis in Journalism Provoke a Crisis in
Democracy?', *Political Quarterly* 73:4 (2002), 400-408, p.405.
5. *The Daily Mail; The Sun*, 22 October 2004.
6. *Invisible Political Actors*, p.7.
7. *Guardian*, 16 and 17 July 2003.
8. Editorial of 1 February 1999, quoted in Stephen Barnett.
9. Oborne and Walters, p.108.
10. *Building Public Value: Renewing the BBC for a Digital World*
(London: BBC, 2004).
11. A YouGov poll for the *Daily Telegraph* in March 2003 found that 14
per cent trusted tabloid journalists to tell the truth, 25 per cent
ministers, 44 per cent their local MP, and 81 per cent BBC news
journalists.
12. *A Question of Trust* (Oxford: Oxford University Press, 2002). See

also *Rethinking Freedom of the Press* (Royal Irish Academy, 2004).

## Chapter Five: Politics and Ideology

1. *Socialist Values and Time*, Fabian Tract 495. See also the 'Footnote to Rally Fellow Socialists' added to the 1982 edition of *In Defence of Politics* and subsequent editions, on which the Fabian publication was based.
2. Anthony Heath and Bridget Taylor, 'New Sources of Abstention', in Geoffrey Evans and Pippa Norris (eds.), *Critical Elections* (London: Sage, 1999), and British Election Study 2001.
3. Figures taken from the British Election Study 2001.
4. For a recent review of literature on the post war consensus see K. Hickson, 'The Post War Consensus Revisted', *Political Quarterly* 75:2, 142-54 (2004).
5. David Marquand, *Decline of the Public* (Cambridge: Polity, 2004), p.59.
6. Otto Kirchheimer, 'The Transformation of the Western European Party Systems', in J. LaPalombara and M. Weiner (eds.), *Political Parties and Party Development* (Princeton: Princeton University Press, 1966), p.200.
7. Michael Jacobs, 'Reason to Believe', *Prospect*, October 2002, 32-37.
8. See http://www.compassonline.org.uk/ and http://www.newwavelabour.co.uk/.
9. '1994 and all that', *Fabian Review*, 116:3 (2004).

## Chapter Six: Politics and Political Parties

1. In 1987 the figure was still 22 per cent. Ivor Crewe, Neil Day and Anthony Fox, *The British Electorate 1963-87: A compendium of data from the British Election Studies* (Cambridge: Cambridge University Press, 1991) and British Social Attitudes survey 2003.
2. British Election Study.
3. Angela Eagle, *A Deeper Democracy* (London: Catalyst, 2003).
4. Wyn Grant, 'Pressure Politics: From "Insider" Politics to Direct Action?', *Parliamentary Affairs*, 54 (2001), 337-348, p.346.
5. These restrictions were moved by the government during the House of Lords' consideration of the bill, following pressure from the Conservative opposition. Both main parties therefore embraced this

approach. However, there were dissenting voices. For example Baroness Gould (herself formerly a senior Labour Party official) said 'I have great difficulty in believing that it is possible to form a commission of people with no basic experience of the job that they are meant to supervise or regulate' (House of Lords Hansard, 11 May 2000, col. 1761).

6. This model has been mooted by theorists such as Kirchheimer (see note above) and Katz and Mair ('Changing Models of Party Organization and Democracy: The Emergence of the Cartel Party', *Party Politics*, 1 [1995], 5-28). It tempted some 'revisionist' Labour politicians such as Crosland in the 1960s, and 'modernisers' in the 1990s. On the latter see for example Dan Clifton, 'The Death of the Mass Party', *Renewal*, 2:2 (1994), 82-87.

7. For the impact of local campaigns see David Denver, Gordon Hands and Iain McAllister, 'The Electoral Impact of Constituency Campaigning in Britain, 1992-2001', *Political Studies* 52:2 (2004), 289-306.

8. See for example Dave Prentis, 'No Hidden Surprises, No Late Extras', *Fabian Review* 115:3 (2003), 14-15; Peter Hain, *The Future Party* (London: Catalyst, 2004); Meg Russell, *Building New Labour: The Politics of Party Organisation* (Basingstoke: Palgrave, 2005).

## Conclusion: Building a New Culture of Politics

1. *In Defence of Politics* (London: Continuum, 2000), p.25.

2. *Guardian*, 8 November 2004

3. For example, the proportion of Scots believing that 'parties are only interested in votes, not opinions' or that it 'doesn't matter which party is in power' have increased since 1997 (Scottish Election Study 1997, Scottish Social Attitudes Survey 1999–2003).